POET

Teshelle Combs

For the little ones with the big talk.
Say the things.

GIRL POET

Teshelle Combs

Age Gap

Underaged.

Underplayed.

Not for drinking.

Just for thinking.

Throw up.

Grow up.

Mind hot.

Gut shot.

Call me when

You're older.

Underaged.

Underpaid.

Not for thinking.

Just for drinking.

You'll always be

A girl.

Moonlighting

Under the desk

When the teacher isn't looking,

I go from a girl

To a dreamer.

Book in lap

And only half listening.

Shhh.

If he finds out

He'll confiscate

me.

Faeries

In the woods after dark

I draw a circle in the leaves.

It's not allowed to make

shapes out of hope

And certainly not in leaves

And not in the woods

And not after dark.

Little girls are meant for

Straight lines with books on heads.

Little girls are meant for very little.

Silhouette

Hey babe,

I'm a tight dress.

Try to take it off

And I vanish in a

Cloud of face powder.

Sexy walker.

Sexy talker.

No arch left

In these heels.

No smack left

In these cheeks.

A girl in red

Wants trouble.

Look, babe.

Don't touch.

Church Girl

I confess.

I liked it when you got mad.

I cursed in my head.

I wore pants on purpose.

I held my hymnal upside down.

I didn't always use the girl's room.

I pretended to forget the words.

And then...in the end...confessed.

Tomboy

There was nothing I wanted more

Than a pair of overalls, one strap off

And a backwards baseball cap.

There was nothing I wanted more

Than to crack my knuckles

And sport Band-Aids on fingertips.

To be less of a girl

And more than a boy.

If You Knew My Mother

Little brother

And me

On a Saturday morning

Grabbing branches

Together.

Great Uncle

Pulls my arm

Hard.

Feet hit the earth.

"Girls don't

Climb trees."

Weaker Sex

Bad at math.

I mean,

Good enough,

For a girl.

Carry the number of people.

Divide and conquer.

Add it all up.

And the remainder

Remains.

I won't be

Saving any

Worlds.

Mix Up

Hilarious

How we got

Hunting and gathering

So wrong.

Ever seen a girl

Find ways to

Tear someone apart?

Let the boys find the berries.

Someone give that woman

A spear.

Get Help

For the girls we called it self-defense.

For the boys we named it art.

We practiced daily,

An arm over my throat and crushing.

Don't hesitate, he said.

Lay him on the ground

And run run run.

Do not try to win.

You will not win.

It is not worth trying.

He was right to tell me

To just get help.

Don't Be Such A Girl

Taking care but not for myself.

Starch the shirts right or at least better.

Never stir the rice when it's boiling.

Learn to sweep without a teacher.

And, for the love of heaven,

Try not to be hysterical.

Girls are known for moods.

Girls are known for swings.

Girls are known hardly enough.

Girls are known too much.

Try not to be such a girl.

Implicit Bias

Straight hair

Is more

Beautiful.

Do not

Comment and say,

Oh no! No! All hair is

Pretty.

You are lying.

We have all

Read the reviews.

Other hair is

Good.

Straight hair

Is better.

I have been a girl

Long enough

To know the difference.

Stern Talkings To

Nothing makes a heart drop

Like being summoned when

You could have just been called.

Wide eyes and cracked lips

Because you have not

Been a good enough girl for

Whoever has been keeping record.

Lime

Girls are best at

Picking through thorns

To find the ripe limes.

Oh, and slicing them up.

Oh, and squeezing them out.

Never mind the

Nonsensical sting

Of tart juice on

Fresh cuts.

The boys will be

Thirsty

After doing whatever it is

They are best at.

Anne

When trapped in

An attic

Indefinitely,

Be sure to bring

Paper and pen.

If no one finds you,

We will find you.

Girls die.

Attics empty.

But words

Turn girls

To words

Turn girls

To words.

I Don't Like Fruit

I don't like fruit,

Goshdarnit.

Not every girl

Wants

Champagne and strawberries.

Not every girl

Wants

You.

I want

Blood spilled

While

Making a way.

Happy has nothing

To do with

Valentine's Day.

And goshdarnit,

I don't like fruit.

Style

Put color

Everywhere you want

And nowhere you don't.

A girl is a prism

Even in the dark.

Feminine Attempt

Heels to the movies.

Strutting up to the ticket counter,

And knowing there is no point

In a girl trying to run.

You Like Pink

You like pink.

This they told me this

On the day of my birth.

Baby girls

Are introduced to

Preferred identity

Before they are

Introduced to

themselves.

No Thank You

Once there was

A boy

Who told

A girl

She was

Stuck up

For a

Let down.

Stick it up,

Girl.

Stick it up.

Submit

Women walk around

Kicking the back of

Girls' knees

Lest they forget

To quiver when

It's required.

Not because we

Are weak.

But because

It is not time

To show we are

Strong.

Needles And Jars

Must life be

A pickle jar

We ask our boys

To open?

Must life be

A torn stitch

We ask out girls

To mend?

Life For A Life

Being held at night

Is more than just

A girl with a wish.

It is implanted

And instinctual

For the survival

Of humankind.

Hold a girl at night

And the world keeps

Turning.

Call Her Home

When you do it right,

There is no safer place

Than in the arms of a

Woman.

A girl needs a

Shelter at night.

And a woman

Makes one.

Burner

Making dinner as a child,

I cooked the meat all the way through.

A small girl playing with fire

And the men expecting no smoke.

Boards

Making dinner as an adult,

I no longer make any meat.

A big girl playing with knives

And the men manning the flame.

Girl Fight

I could have been a legend

Had I learned to break a board.

But I was a young girl

And he was hands on.

If something must break,

It will never be me.

Mirror Child

Four years old

And shoving the tissues away.

I want to see them.

Trace tears in canyons down my face.

Something about a girl.

Beauty is unmatched when taken away.

Grown Up Girl

I am in training

To be a

Functional adult.

Takes a bit of

Uncertainty and

A lot of

Arrogance

To be a girl

Who pays taxes and

Pretends she's always

okay.

Toning

Text me

But please don't call.

I need to unhear

The crack in your voice.

I need to cancel the pauses.

I need to not have

You pressed to my ear

And me waiting.

Girls are born in the

Cracks

In the pauses

In the pressing

In the waiting.

Please, don't call me.

Text.

Compass Rose

I do the choosing

Even though you offer the choices.

You say I am a girl,

But I decide what it means.

When It Comes

Late night crying

With Netflix in my ears.

Girls on the other end

In the process of some

On screen betrayal.

Tears like oil down my nose

And make sure not to move.

Anointed and bearing the weight.

I don't know where the sadness

Comes from when it comes.

But it comes

Late at night

Both ways.

Closet Shadows

They do not lurk.

They dwell.

Perfectly comfortable

In their quarantine.

Maybe they find

Their power in the

Times I've pulled

Self hate off hangers

And stuffed myself

Into compromises.

Size 12. Size 4. Size 9.

Well clad in the dark.

The shoes make

The girl.

I suppose I am

Closet shadows.

In school

I got real loud

During my

Hamlet monologue.

I still don't know

What i was saying,

But a girl with

A book

Had the floor.

Might as well

Shake the walls.

Sat down to

Wrinkled brows

And frowns.

I used my smirk

As a

Bookmark.

And Scene

Unsalaried

First job. Landscaping.

Shovel. Pickaxe.

Eating weeds.

My dad: "Landscaping is

A good first job for

A girl."

To teach me what?

To teach me who?

Now I know.

It was to teach them.

Inside Work

Where I'm from

Girls do

Inside work.

Sweep.

Wipe.

Stir.

Mend.

Store.

Talk a little.

Hint a little.

Taste a little.

While the boys are

out.

We keep our secrets

Just like our work.

Inside.

The Day My Books Were Gone

The day my books were gone

I ravaged the house.

Pushed the couches.

Upended the drawers.

My mother said she threw them out.

That day I knew what it meant

To have been a girl.

Media Room

In middle school

The girls used the library for

Not books.

Don't they know

The pages

Are for storing?

Don't they know

The binding holds

Every secret it finds?

Don't they know

A good story

Never forgets

What it knows?

I Know Your Name

Shame

Is something

Made just for

Girls

Who know

Better

Than boys

Who know

better.

How Young Is Too Young

Grown men in their trucks

Roll their windows down, old school.

Ask if we girls in our school uniforms

Want a ride to their houses.

We say no, but with confidence.

If we tremor, they will know they are winning.

They drive slow beside us

And we pretend they do not.

We girls, in our uniforms,

Hold tight to still just being girls.

With Wine

Hahahahaha.

The women laugh all together

At a thing called 'Girls Night.'

Their nails click on their glasses

And their lips are sticky with color.

I am an alien in a perfumed land.

Hahaha.

Who are these people?

And goodness, who am I?

In Training

The effort it takes

To be properly

A girl.

Well shaven.

Well read.

Well dressed.

Well mannered.

Well maintained.

And unsure of the last time

One was actually

well.

Just Coarse

In the back of a van

Late at night

A boy told me

His sisters had

Hair like cotton

And mine was

Made of silk.

I will remember

What it is like

To know someone

Lied to me

And for me to

Believe it anyway.

If I have to be a girl,

Cotton hair will do

Just fine.

No Spectators

The sport of kissing

Is one that makes

Little revenue.

To play, a boy

And a girl

Use their lips

To forge false accords.

Whoever breaks first is the winner.

Whoever breaks first is the loser.

Someone always breaks first.

What We Could Be

Against a coconut tree

On the beach nearest my house

You said we could be

Friends with benefits.

It was the last time we spoke.

I remember sometimes

How you wanted to trade

A girl for a kiss,

When you could have had

Both.

Like You Like It

What you see

Is what you want to see.

A mood. A smile. A straight line. A fluid puddle.

A girl is viewed through the slanting of

Scaled eyes.

You pull and push and rip and arrange.

But you will never see

What you want to see.

Rather, you will behold what you've made of her.

A girl.

Just like you like it.

Sticks

I like sticks not flowers.

The wonder of a woman who

Holds on to old things.

The glory of a girl with

A stern grasp.

I grip you in my hands

And set you in my vase.

Up to you whether you'll

Whither or weather.

PreSchool

When I learned I owned the ocean

I was still young.

Before I knew what small was.

I could inhale and the

Expanse flooded my chest.

Sprint to the edge of it and

Have it kiss my ankles.

Or stand on the mountain

And look out with my chin up.

A gentle thought passing between us.

You are mine.

Back when a girl was not yet me.

Back when I was still young.

Back when I owned

The whole damn thing.

And Brown

Many, Many a time

I have stood back and

Cursed

At whoever decided to make me

Small

And smart

And weak

And brave

And a girl

And brown.

Proprietary

I have so many brothers

Who loved me.

Girls don't get to keep things.

Barefoot Feminist

Now that I am old

I know the secret

We almost forgot.

Trade broken arches

For toes in the dirt.

They will tell you

Girls should be careful.

But joke is on them.

No shoes.

No service.

Splinter Name

White girl.

The name put

Splinters in my brain.

If I am *white girl*

Then who are they?

And why am I not us?

We each have one—

A splinter name.

Don't tell me yours.

I cannot help you.

I am not the us

You want to be

Part of.

Gambling

In college

Where we make mistakes

And not our beds

And too many bets—

A boy kissed my forehead,

Trying to get me on

One of those

Plastic mattresses.

It was a bet,

I found out.

In these places,

A girl

Is not a friend.

A girl is

a bet.

Something is expected

In return.

Horse Girl

Ride a beast

When you feel powerless.

See that there is someone

Wild and big and free

Who could crush any man

underfoot

But has chosen to be

With a girl

For a time.

Makers

When we have children

We know something knew.

A girl is not a plaything

Even if you treat her like one.

We

Cannot

Be

Broken.

It is a quiet truth

Passed in hushed breath

And in a tight grip, palm to palm.

Combs

Shut up and get some ice.

Shut up and hold her elbows.

A woman can tell when someone is

About to change the whole world

Even if you treat her like she can't.

The truth, like a current under the

Tiles or the roots or the carpets or dirt, before the
Baby even screams:

We cannot be broken;

We are the makers.

Pen

Sword in hand and narrowed eyes

And the whole world shall kneel.

I am no girl, no woman, no mortal.

I am Master

Of the

Pen.

Nothing is unless I say so.

Nothing goes unless I say no.

So beware. Be careful. Be mine.

Zamyr

Girl who sings

Low mournful tones

When the casket rolls in.

Girl who sings

Soaring notes

When the worship lifts.

Girl who sings

Smoke and honey

When the vows are made.

Who will sing

For you?

Ball/Chain

I traded

My last name

For a chance

At a new one.

Life is nothing

If not a risk,

Leaning forward

Eyes wide open.

Take the girl

And she will be

The one who takes you.

I traded my last name

For a pair

Of wings

Like no one has

Ever seen.

Eny

My grandmother.

Destiny commander.

Was never a girl.

Not ever.

She was born

Just as she is now.

Ninety-eight

And hard as stones.

It has gone

Exactly how she

Meant it to.

On the phone

She stares with one glance.

You are still

A little child.

At least

She did not

Call me

A

Girl.

More Works by Teshelle Combs

Let There Be Nine: Enneagram Poetry

For Her

Words laced together on behalf of an idea, a place, a world. Poems for the earth, from someone who's lived here all her life. Poems about what it takes to bring life out of death.

For Him

Words assorted for the robust, for the place we love. Poems about the bold and unafraid nature of nature.

For Them

Poems about the turning of the earth, towards and away from one thing to another, and for the idea of "them," from which we also turn away or towards.

For Us

Poems about the delicate fearlessness of the earth and its beginnings and endings. Perhaps it will give these to us if we are up for the learning.

Love Bad
Poems About Love. Not Love Poems.

A book of poems, by me, Teshelle Combs, for the purpose of the investigation of, or rather the accusation of, or rather the commendation of love and all its claims on me. I would say enjoy, but I am trying to be less naive these days.

Love Bad More
Poems About Love. More Or Less.

A continuation of poems about love by me, Teshelle Combs, in honor of the continuous nature of love and how it goes in either direction, regardless of our requests. I hope this book finds you out of control.

Love Bad Best
Poems About Love. Last, Not Best.

The final installment of poems about love, by me, Teshelle Combs, unless there will be more, which is either up to me or up to love, but probably not up to any of us if poetry has anything to do with anything. You are welcome to it, but I would advise a tentative approach.

Breath Like Glass

Poems for love that never lasts.

CORE SERIES

Ava is the kind of girl who knows what's real and what isn't. Nothing in life is fair. Nothing is given freely. Nothing is painless. Every foster kid can attest to those truths, and Ava lives them every day. But when she meets a family of dragon shifters and is chosen to join them as a rider, her very notion of reality is shaken. She doesn't believe she can let her guard down. She doesn't think she can let them in—especially not the reckless, kind-eyed Cale. To say yes to him means he would be hers—her dragon and her companion—for life. But what if Ava has no life left to give?

The System Series

1 + 1 = Dead. That's the only math that adds up when you're in the System. Everywhere Nick turns, he's surrounded by the inevitability of his own demise at the hands of the people who stole his life from him. That is, until those hands deliver the bleeding, feisty, eye-rolling Nessa Parker. Tasked with keeping his new partner alive, Nick must face all the ways he's died and all the things he's forgotten.

Nessa might as well give up. The moment she gets into that car, the moment she lays her hazel eyes on her new partner, her end begins. It doesn't matter that Nick Masters can slip through time by computing mathematical algorithms in his mind. It doesn't matter how dark and handsome and irresistibly cold he is. Nessa has to defeat her own shadows. Together and alone, Nick and Nessa make sense of their senseless fates and fight for the courage to change it all. Even if it means the System wins and they end up...well...dead.

Contact Teshelle Combs

Instagram @TeshelleCombs

Email: teshellecombs@gmail.com

Acknowledgments

Thank you to every girl, every woman, every boy, every man, every fluid heart and every mortal who dares to be alive in this world. You are seen. Thank you for reading. May it all become what it is meant to be, and may the future you make be good.